When Cats Assasinate

Produced in 2005 by
PRC Publishing
The Chrysalis Building
Bramley Road, London W10 6SP

An imprint of **Chrysalis** Books Group plc

ISBN 1 85648 771 7

Printed and bound in China

When Cats Assasinate

David W. Watts & Andrew Davies

PRC

Contents

Historical Hits

Cats have never liked dogs.

It's a rivalry that goes back a long, long way. Even in the time of Rameses and King Tutankhamun, Egyptians noticed that cats had it in for dogs. A few drops of arsenic placed under a claw and a quick swipe when courtiers weren't looking was all it needed to establish their supremacy.

From Roman times to medieval times, cats used their superior brain power to outwit dogs.

"Look it's called a catapault, not a dogapault, okay?"

Sailors in the British navy lived in fear of "a dose of the cat" – the terrifying cat o' nine tails certainly shivered a few timbers as it enforced a brutal discipline on scurvy dogs. Few realised that the back-flogging whip with nine strands was named after (Mad) Moggee McGee, deadliest cut-throat on the Western main.

In the twentieth century cats have used loopholes in the law to continue their deadly reign of terror against dogs. In America, the National Rifle Association for Cats discovered an error in the constititution. The U.S. constitution gives citizens the right to bear arms, but in an earlier signed draft, it actually said every citizen has the right to arm bears. Cats argued that if bears, who are sometimes too stupid even to open litter bins, were allowed automatic weapons, then they should have them too. Dogs never pressed their claim.

Thus there have been some dark days in politics when cats have picked out high profile targets.

Through the 60s and 70s cats used a variety of weapons to control and silence opposition from dogs. Organised crime employed a number of hit kitties such as Baby-Faced Paws Portillo whose speciality was to hide in a delicious dish of Meaty Chunks, that really was "to die for."

Killer Kitties
Some Simple Strategies

Eliminating a "wetnose" is easy. Dogs are stupid. Doing it with style, though, takes class.

Taking a dog-nap is not a good idea when your wake-up call is 9mm wide.

Sometimes, all you
need to do is remove
the pin and shout

"Catch, boy!"

They're complete
suckers for a
thrown bone.

In the South, good ol'boy cats with a mean at-it-tood, load up a six-pack of beer, get in the pick-up and go git themselves some dawg.

Silent and deadly. Never underestimate the power of a ginger tom. Now he can make himself a lovely...

...dog rug. It's the feline equivalent of the fur coat.

Every right-thinking feeling feline wants a dog rug to call their own.

Bleached retriever is so "in" this season.

The Opportunist Killer

Sometimes they just have to be in the right place at the right time...

...to give a helping paw...

...a nudge in the
right direction...

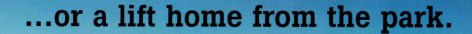

...or a lift home from the park.

Sly Felines

Dogs are too trusting for their own good. They'll believe anything you tell them. And they can never spot danger ahead.

This dog thought he was on an alpine bone hunt.

THIN ICE
GO AHEAD... TRY IT
ANYWAY... YOU DON'T
WEIGH THAT
MUCH... IT
WON'T
BREAK

This pack of eager huskies had no idea they were treading on thin ice.

While the sign on the outside of this catflap reads:

FREE DOG FOOD INSIDE

Macabre Moggies

They say that a dog is a man's best friend. That's probably because men don't like complex relationships.

However, cats are jealous creatures – they cannot forgive or forget.

Or stand to see a dog having a good time on theme park thrill rides.

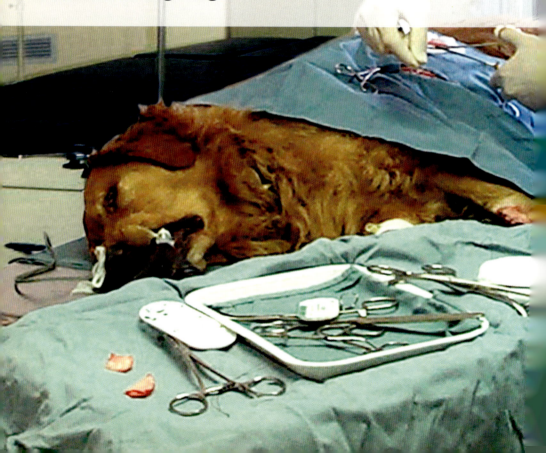

The success rate for cat-assisted veterinary operations is not encouraging.

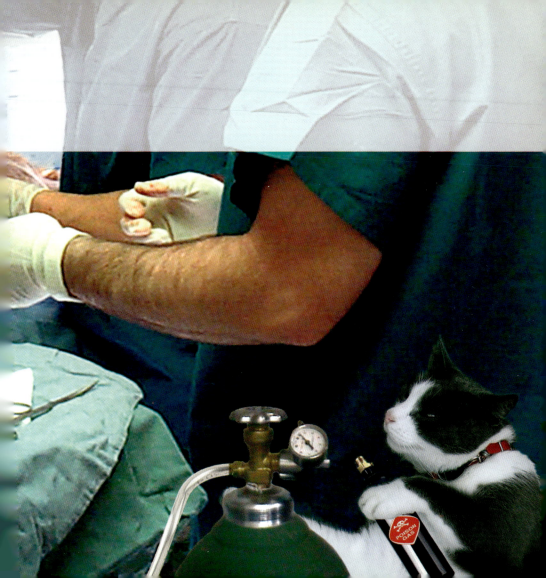

While cats who run boarding kennels don't get many return bookings.

And take a pooch to certain grooming parlours and it won't stand a cat in hell's chance of making it to the dog show. Unless it's in a tin.

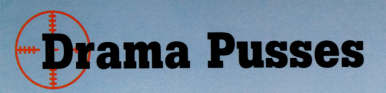

Drama Pusses

How about a water-skiing ride of a lifetime in crocodile-infested waters.

No, it's not difficult sending Fido to that great boneyard in the sky. But if he's got to go, it might as well be with a **BANG** or a **SPLAT** or a **KER-BOOM!**

A short vacation
down on the farm.

A relaxing stroll along the beach.

Oopsie,

mind those dog-sensitive landmines.

Sometimes a cat on the hard shoulder is just too tempting for truckies.

Though a bit of mechanical assistance never went amiss.

Skydiving is a whole lot more interesting without parachutes.

And woodworking can be a relaxing hobby with some great knick-knacks to show off round the home afterwards.

Cats object to the phrase,

"It's raining cats and dogs."

Raining dogs is just fine by them.

Torture

Some cats have a cruel streak a mile wide.

"Okay, golden paws, how do you make a dog go

WOOF!...?"

Curiosity may not kill cats, but it does lead to interesting experiments with domestic appliances...

Dogs love digging big holes. Sometimes they're just a little too big.

And they love entertaining friends.

"Hot dog anyone..?"

Comedy Killers

Never let it be said that cats don't possess a sense of humour.

They're big fans of the Roadrunner cartoons.

And Tom and Jerry.

The radio-controlled stick
has batteries that can last up
to nine hours.

Enough to drown three large dogs or seven very small ones.

They have an endless love of practical jokes...

DOGS NEEDED
FOR SPECTACULAR
CIRCUS ACT
NO EXPERIENCE REQUIRED

Tkdf dfknvg lerger rger aergege oger tdfmgm aokgergrg arkg eakgfer adlrgm fmg fgqfh shhfhh slfs,fkk huky dygdytyya srthsrthhsrt ylhsrtylh fohhsfh sfhhvh sfehm

...and the electric lamp-post is
the one they love best.

Copy-Cat Slayings

Cinema has been the inspiration for many of their dog disposal methods.

Right from the early days of the silent movies, cats were inspired to tie dogs to train tracks.

They started to copy spy
movies like the Bond classics.

Mob flicks like *The Godfather*, Don Woofilo sleeps with the fishes.

Action films, like
Where Eagles Dare.

Meet The Fockers spawned a wave of copy-cat killings.

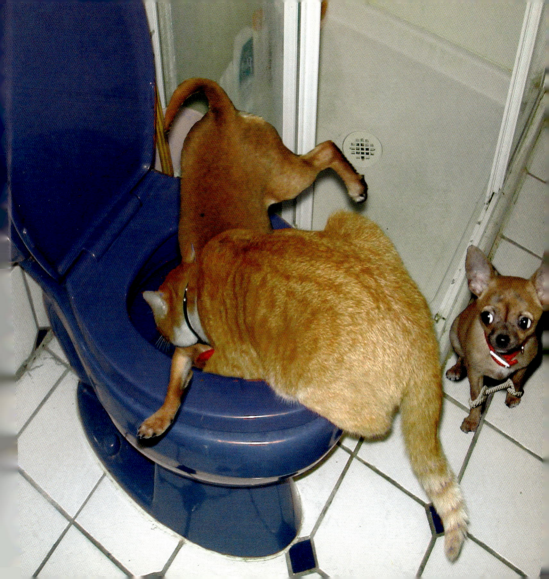

And perhaps the deadliest of them all – *The Pup Terminator.*

Acknowledgments

The authors would like to thank the Chrysalis Image Library for the loan of the "Chairman Miaow" photo sessions; also the friends and family who loaned them innumerable cat and dog pictures, including pictures of: Rosie, Rosie's second litter, Mittens, Mouse, Paws, Puddy, Dolly, Bagpuss, Mitch, Genghis, Soots, Bungee, Marmalade, Tigger, Thunderball, Prince, Snorkel, Patch, Toby, Pipe, Elvis, Woody, Bill and Barney.

Mr. Watts can confirm that no cats were taught techniques they might use elsewhere in copy-cat killings, and anyway, the cats weren't that interested.

Mr Watts and Mr Davies would like to add that they are both huge dog lovers. But more in the way that Koreans love dogs.